P9-DMV-155

First Facts®

Spotlight on the Continents

SPOTLIGHT ON
NORTH AMERICA

by Karen Bush Gibson

CAPSTONE PRESS
a capstone imprint

First Facts is published by Capstone Press,
151 Good Counsel Drive, P.O. Box 669, Mankato, Minnesota 56002.
www.capstonepub.com

 Books published by Capstone Press are manufactured with paper
containing at least 10 percent post-consumer waste.

Library of Congress Cataloging-in-Publication Data
Gibson, Karen Bush.
  Spotlight on North America / by Karen Bush Gibson.
     p. cm.—(First facts. Spotlight on the continents)
  Summary: "An introduction to North America including climate, landforms, plants,
animals, and people"—Provided by publisher.
  Includes bibliographical references and index.
  ISBN 978-1-4296-6621-3 (library binding)
  1. North America—Juvenile literature. I. Title. II. Series.
  E38.5.G53 2011
  970—dc22   2010037112

Editorial Credits
Lori Shores, editor; Gene Bentdahl, designer; Laura Manthe, production specialist

Photo Credits
Alamy/David Grossman, 16; Jim Parkin, 20
Corel, 14 (bottom)
DigitalVision, 9 (top and bottom left), 14 (top left)
Photodisc, 1
Shutterstock/Olivier Le Queinec, cover; ARTSILENSEcom, 13; Clayton Thacker, 12;
     Mark R, 18; nikitsin, 19; PixAchi, 9 (bottom right); S.R. Maglione, 14 (top right)

Artistic Effects
Shutterstock/seed

Essential content terms are **bold** and are defined at the bottom of the page
where they first appear.

Printed in the United States of America in Melrose Park, Illinois.
092010   005935LKS11

TABLE OF CONTENTS

CONTINENTS OF THE WORLD

NORTH AMERICA

North America has everything from ice-covered islands to steamy **rain forests**. This huge landmass is the world's third largest **continent**.

Most people came to North America in the last 400 years. Today about 538 million people call North America home.

rain forest—a thick forest where a great deal of rain falls

continent—one of Earth's seven large landmasses

FAST FACTS ABOUT
NORTH AMERICA

🌐 **Size:** 9,352,000 square miles
(24,221,569 square kilometers)

🌐 **Number of countries:** 23

🌐 **Highest point:** Mount McKinley,
Alaska, 20,320 feet (6,194 meters)
above sea level

🌐 **Lowest point:** Death Valley, California,
282 feet (86 meters) below sea level

🌐 **Largest cities:** Mexico City, Mexico;
New York City, United States;
Toronto, Canada

🌐 **Longest river:** Mississippi River,
2,340 miles (3,766 kilometers) long

COUNTRIES OF NORTH AMERICA

ARCTIC OCEAN

GREENLAND (DENMARK)

UNITED STATES (ALASKA)

CANADA

PACIFIC OCEAN

UNITED STATES

ATLANTIC OCEAN

MEXICO

UNITED STATES (HAWAII)

THE BAHAMAS

HAITI

CUBA

DOMINICAN REPUBLIC

PUERTO RICO

VIRGIN ISLANDS (U.S.)

BRITISH VIRGIN ISLANDS (U.K.)

ST. KITTS-NEVIS

JAMAICA

BELIZE

HONDURAS

DOMINICA

ANTIGUA & BARBUDA

GUATEMALA

ST. VINCENT & THE GRENADINES

ST. LUCIA

EL SALVADOR

NICARAGUA

GRENADA

BARBADOS

PANAMA

TRINIDAD & TOBAGO

COSTA RICA

N W E S

Kilometers
0   500   1000

0   620
Miles

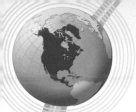

CLIMATE

North America has every type of **climate**. Much of the continent has four seasons. Cold winters give way to brisk springs. Then come warm summers and cool fall days. But northern areas are usually freezing cold. Southern areas stay warm and wet all year.

climate—the usual weather that occurs in a place

LANDFORMS OF NORTH AMERICA

ARCTIC
OCEAN

Bering Sea

Yukon River

Mt. McKinley
20,320 feet
(6,194 meters)

Great
Bear Lake

Mackenzie River

Great
Slave Lake

Labrador Sea

Hudson Bay

PACIFIC
OCEAN

Fraser River

Saskatchewan River

Nelson River

G R E A T   P L A I N S

Lake Winnipeg

Snake River

Missouri River

Lake
Superior

St. Lawrence River

Lake
Huron

ROCKY MOUNTAINS

Platte River

Lake
Michigan

Lake
Erie

Lake
Ontario

APPALACHIAN MOUNTAINS

Great Basin

Mississippi River

Ohio River

Colorado River

Arkansas River

Tennessee River

N
W   E
S

Rio Grande River

Mississippi River

ATLANTIC
OCEAN

LEGEND
▲ highest point
▨ mountains
⌒ river

Gulf of Mexico

Kilometers
0 200 400 600 800 1000

0   200   400   600
Miles

Caribbean Sea

SOUTH
AMERICA

LANDFORMS

North America has many lakes, rivers, and mountains. Ships carry goods across the Great Lakes. Water flows in the long Mississippi River. Other rivers cut across the Appalachian and Rocky Mountains to the Mississippi.

Deserts and plains cover parts of North America. Winds blow across the western Great Basin's dry land. The Great Plains blanket the central United States.

PLANTS

Farmers grow many **crops** in North America. About one-third of the world's soybeans grow on this continent. Wheat, cotton, and fruit also grow here.

Paper and other goods are made from trees that fill forests in Canada and the United States. Mahogany trees from southern rain forests are used to make furniture.

crop—a plant grown in large amounts and that is often used for food

ANIMALS

Climate determines where animals live in North America. Polar bears and caribou live in the cold north. Cougars hunt in the southern rain forests. Hot, dry deserts are home to Gila monsters. Bison roam the **temperate** Great Plains.

temperate—having a mild climate

POPULATION DENSITY OF NORTH AMERICA

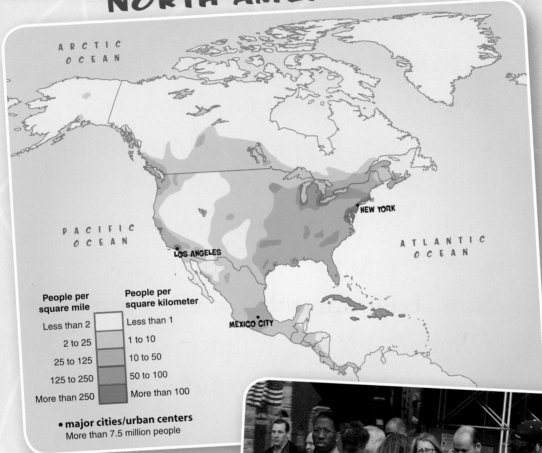

ARCTIC OCEAN

PACIFIC OCEAN

ATLANTIC OCEAN

NEW YORK

LOS ANGELES

MEXICO CITY

People per square mile	People per square kilometer
Less than 2	Less than 1
2 to 25	1 to 10
25 to 125	10 to 50
125 to 250	50 to 100
More than 250	More than 100

• major cities/urban centers
More than 7.5 million people

PEOPLE

People in North America come from many **cultures**. They have different languages and religions. Most North Americans speak English. Spanish is the second most used language. Christianity is the most common religion. But Judaism, Islam, and other religions are also practiced in North America.

culture—a people's way of life, ideas, customs, and traditions

LIVING IN NORTH AMERICA

North American homes and clothing change with the climate. Flat roofs keep houses cool in the south. People keep cool by wearing cotton clothing.

In the north, melting snow drips off slanted roofs. People wear coats and gloves to stay warm in winter.

NORTH AMERICA AND THE WORLD

Many countries buy wood, food, and minerals from North America. This continent's forests provide large amounts of wood. North Americans also grow some of the world's food. Minerals, such as copper, nickel, and silver, are sent worldwide.

GLOSSARY

climate (KLY-muht)—the usual weather that occurs in a place

continent (KAHN-tuh-nuhnt)—one of Earth's seven large landmasses

crop (KROP)—a plant grown in large amounts and that is often used for food

culture (KUHL-chuhr)—a people's way of life, ideas, customs, and traditions

rain forest (RAYN FOR-ist)—a thick forest where a great deal of rain falls

temperate (TEM-pur-it)—having a mild climate

READ MORE

Aloian, Molly and Bobbie Kalman. *Explore North America.* Explore the Continents. New York: Crabtree Pub., 2007.

Foster, Karen. *Atlas of North America.* World Atlases. Minneapolis: Picture Window Books, 2008.

INTERNET SITES

FactHound offers a safe, fun way to find Internet sites related to this book. All of the sites on FactHound have been researched by our staff.

Here's all you do:

Visit *www.facthound.com*

Type in this code: 9781429666213

Super-cool stuff! Check out projects, games and lots more at
www.capstonekids.com

INDEX